101 RECEIVER DRILLS

Stan Zweifel

ISBN: 1-57167-191-9
Library of Congress Catalog Card Number: 97-69609

Book Design: Michelle Summers
Cover Design: Deborah M. Bellaire
Front Cover Photos: David Gonzales
Developmental Editor: David Hamburg
Illustrations: David Mendez

Coaches Choice Books is a division of: Sagamore Publishing, Inc.
                                             P.O. Box 647
                                             Champaign, IL 61824-0647
                                             Web Site: http//www.sagamorepub.com

DEDICATION

This book is dedicated to my loving family—Diane,
my wife of 23 years; my daughters, Saree and
Shannon; and my sons, Michael and Mark.

ACKNOWLEDGMENTS

I would like to acknowledge all the players and coaches with whom I have had the opportunity to work over the years. Their efforts and commitment to the great game of football have been an inspiration to me.

I would also like to thank the staff at Coaches Choice books, in particular Michelle Summers and David Hamburg for enabling the project to come to completion.

CONTENTS

Chapter

PREFACE

The *101 Receiver Drills* book has been written for coaches and athletes at all competitive levels. Each of the 101 drills was selected for its ability to provide the coach with an effective learning environment for the fundamental skills and techniques attendant to receiver play.

For organizational purposes, the drills have been placed in one of nine chapters according to the primary developmental focus of the drill. Each drill offers football coaches a terrific teaching tool for providing their receivers with the requisite attributes for success. Many of the drills, however, involve more than one unique skill and address more than one aspect of receiver play. As a result, each coach should keep an open mind when incorporating these drills into his overall training program. Whenever necessary, he can make adjustments in the method he uses for conducting a drill in order to make that particular drill more appropriate for his specific situation.

The important point to remember is that the considered use of the drills presented in this book can have a positive impact on the success of a football team. Repetition and feedback are two of the key factors which will determine the extent of the effect that these drills will have. As a general rule, the drills are most effective when they are performed regularly as an integral part of a team's training program. A football coach can enhance the effectiveness of each drill by taking steps to ensure that each participant in a drill is given clear and immediate feedback regarding his performance in the drill.

CHAPTER 1

WARM-UP DRILLS

Drill #1: Ball-Handling Drills

Objective: To provide an effective warm-up and teach the fundamentals of agility, foot quickness, and reactions.

Description:

1. Air Dribble (refer to illustration): A receiver should hold the ball on the fat part of the ball and completely release the ball. He should catch the ball before it drops to the ground, continue performing this drill for 30 seconds, and then repeat it with the opposite hand. To build confidence, beginning players should not dribble too fast. They can increase their speed with practice.

2. Finger Roll (refer to illustration): A receiver should hold the ball at one end, with the ball below the hand. The ball should be rolled over on its back so that it sits on top of the hand with the palm still facing down. The ball should then be returned to its original position. This drill should be performed for at least one minute.

3. Hand Circle (refer to illustration): The ball is held like it is in the air dribble drill. The ball should be dropped as the receiver lifts it slightly. The receiver should circle his hand around the ball and grab it in the original position. This technique should be repeated several times.

4. Hand Roll (refer to illustration): The ball should be held at one end, with the palm of the hand down and the ball line perpendicular to the arm/hand line. The ball will then be rolled over the back of the hand and the receiver should grab it by the other end and return it to the original position. This technique should be repeated several times.

5. Wrist Flip and Catch: The receiver holds the ball above his head, flips the ball upwards in a direction opposite the hand movement, and catches it.

6. Globetrotter: The object of this drill is to keep the ball moving as fast as possible and in as many different movement patterns as possible. These movements can include between the legs, around the knees, around the waist, behind the back, around the head, etc. The receiver should try to keep the ball moving as fast as possible for 30 seconds.

7. Juggling: The receiver takes two balls and juggles them in one hand (the throwing hand).

8. Hand-to-Hand: The receiver should pass the ball from hand to hand, quickly catching and tossing the ball. The receiver should also practice these movements behind his back.

9. Ball Security: The ball should be picked up and handled with no air between the body and the ball. The idea is to cover the ball as fast as possible. The receiver should get into his ball-carrying position and have another player poke at the ball and try to jar it loose.

Coaching Points:

•   These drills will help players develop a feel for the football and proper hand-eye coordination.

•   Players will also learn proper positioning of their hands when they are catching the football.

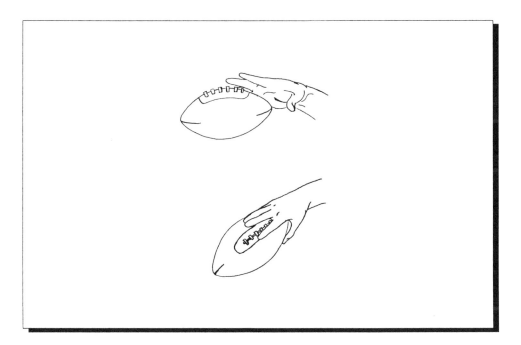

Air Dribble

Finger Roll

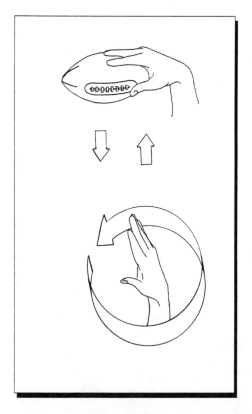

Hand Circle

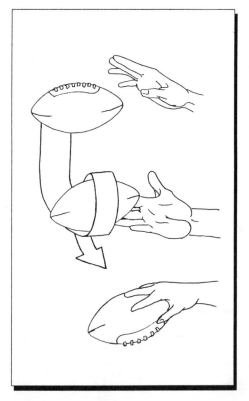

Hand Roll

Drill #2: Start Drill

Objective: To provide an effective warm-up and teach the fundamentals of agility, foot quickness, and reactions.

Description: Defensive players will be positioned behind the receivers. When the coach yells, "Hike!" the receivers should start running. With their heads cocked, they should be able to see the defensive players in their peripheral vision.

Coaching Point:

- The coach should make sure the receivers explode off the line of scrimmage.

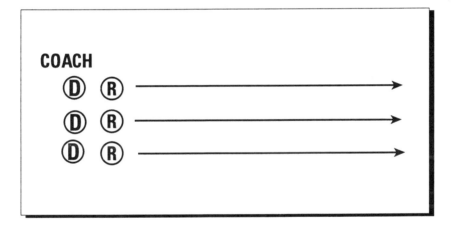

Drill #3: Weave Drill

Objective: To provide an effective warm-up and teach the fundamentals of agility, foot quickness, and reactions.

Description: The receiver will run a route down the field. By using a lateral position, the receiver will force the defensive player to change position. The receiver will use two-on-one backpedalling while the defensive player runs at his shoulders.

Coaching Point:

- This drill is an effective way to teach receivers rhythm.

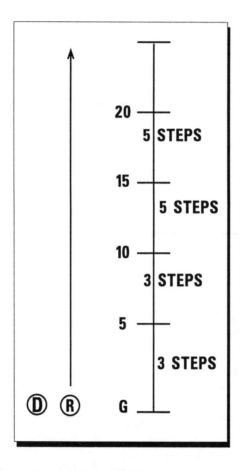

Drill #4: Stance and Starts Drills

Objective: To provide an effective warm-up and teach the fundamentals of agility, foot quickness, and reactions.

Description: The receiver takes his stance and performs 10 five-yard starts at half his normal speed.

Coaching Points:

- Players should use proper execution on the take-off and avoid false steps.

- Players should build up from 50% speed to 80% speed.

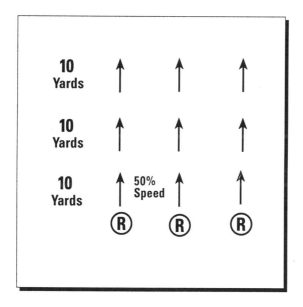

Drill #5: Start/Stop Drill

Objective: To provide an effective warm-up and teach the fundamentals of agility, foot quickness, and reactions.

Description: The receiver runs sideline cuts at five-yard intervals to the right, to the left, back to the right, etc. The procedure should then be reversed, with the receiver coming back to the starting position. Emphasis should be placed on footwork, snapping the head around quickly to look for the ball, staying low in the cut, and working off the foot that's opposite the side of the pattern.

Coaching Points:

- Unnecessary steps should be eliminated.

- The receiver should perform this drill for one minute.

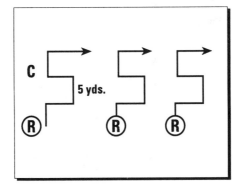

Drill #6: Two-Handed Catch Drill

Objective: To provide an effective warm-up and teach the fundamentals of agility, foot quickness, and reactions.

Description: The receiver looks over his left shoulder and catches the ball in both hands while jogging about 10 yards.

Coaching Points:

- The ball should be caught at the highest point possible with proper hand technique.

- Receivers should execute a catch-cap-lock with the ball.

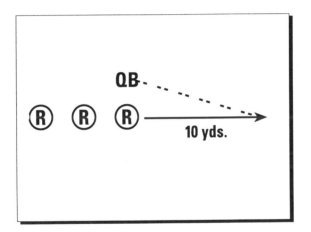

Drill #7: Jump-Turn Drill

Objective: To provide an effective warm-up and teach the fundamentals of agility, foot quickness, and reactions.

Description: From a normal stance the receiver should come off the line of scrimmage at full speed. After running 10 yards he makes a half-twist leaping turn. When he is back on the ground he backpedals for five yards and carioca steps for another five yards.

Coaching Point:

- The receiver's jump should be high and timed so that he does not lean backwards.

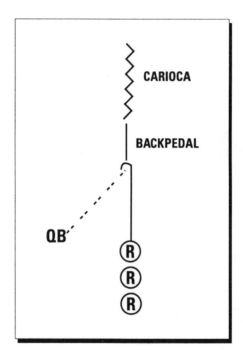

Drill #8: Quick-Turn Drill

Objective: To provide an effective warm-up and teach the fundamentals of agility, foot quickness, and reactions.

Description: From a normal stance the receiver will sprint. On command he should leap and make a complete twist. The twist is made to the left and then to the right. By dipping his shoulder during the spin, the receiver will maintain forward body lean.

Coaching Point:

• This drill should be performed at varying speeds.

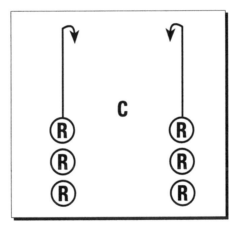

Drill #9: Coil-Run Drill

Objective: To provide an effective warm-up and teach the fundamentals of agility, foot quickness, and reactions.

Description: The receiver makes alternating left and right cuts while running the width of the field between yard lines. The cuts should be made off a bent knee to (1) prevent the defense from reading it, and (2) to develop stability by lowering the receiver's center of gravity so that he may absorb the impact of the cut.

Coaching Point:

• This drill is designed to teach the receiver the importance of making sharp cuts.

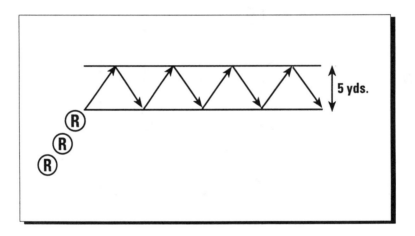

Drill #10: Balance-Run Drill

Objective: To provide an effective warm-up and teach the fundamentals of agility, foot quickness, and reactions.

Description: From a normal stance the receiver sprints 10 yards and, while still running quickly, places his right hand flat on the ground, pushes off, and regains his balance. Without stopping, the receiver should sprint another five yards and place his left hand flat on the ground, push off, and regain his balance. Again, without stopping, he sprints five more yards and places both hands flat on the ground, pushes off, and regains his balance and finishes with a five-yard sprint.

Coaching Points:

- The receiver's body weight should be on his down hand.

- To regain balance, the receiver's leg drive should occur at the same time as the hand push-off.

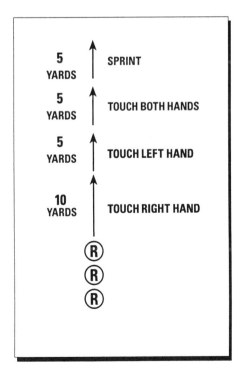

Drill #11: Weave Drill

Objective: To provide an effective warm-up and teach the fundamentals of agility, foot quickness, and reactions.

Description: A three-step weave will give a receiver practice in changing direction with his outside leg. The receiver should start out jogging, then begin striding, and eventually end up running, making sharp 45-degree changes of direction on every third step. The receiver should hold his shoulders square with an imaginary goal line. He should take his third step well outside his center of gravity in order to maintain leverage while moving his center of gravity.

Coaching Point:

- Receivers should use a snaking movement instead of a sharp zig-zag movement.

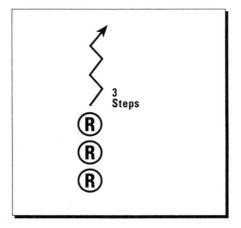

CHAPTER 2

RELEASE DRILLS

Drill #12: Drift Drill

Objective: To develop drift skills for avoiding a restraining defender.

Description: The coach signals for the receiver to drift either to the left or to the right. The defender will attempt to restrain the receiver.

Coaching Points:

- Receivers should try to avoid contact with the defender.

- Receivers should also work on their stances and their releases.

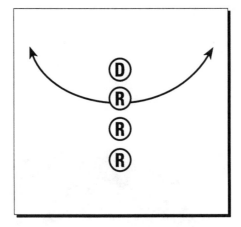

Drill #13: Fake-Out Drill

Objective: To develop faking techniques for avoiding a restraining defender.

Description: The coach signals for the receiver to drift either to the left or to the right. The receiver should react accordingly by faking in one direction and then drifting in the other direction.

Coaching Points:

- A receiver should use a head fake to avoid contact with the defender.

- Receivers should work on different shoulder and head combinations.

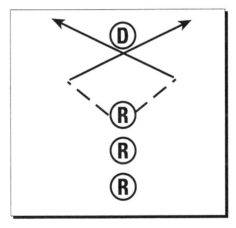

Drill #14: Spin-Out Drill

Objective: To teach how a spinning release will help in avoiding a restraining defender.

Description: On signal from the coach, the receiver should release to the right or to the left of the defender and then spin around and out in the opposite direction.

Coaching Points:

- The receiver should make contact with the defender and then make a spin to escape from that player.

- A tight end should use a bust technique.

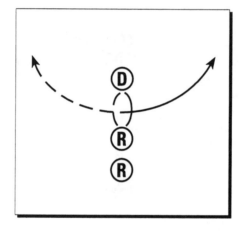

Drill #15: Blast-Out Drill

Objective: To teach the use of an aggressive release directly over a restraining defender.

Description: On signal from the coach, the receiver should step into the defender and deliver a forearm blow. The receiver should then regain body balance and proceed on the pattern.

Coaching Points:

- The defender should be stunned by the initial blow from the receiver.

- An additional escape technique should be incorporated with the forearm blow.

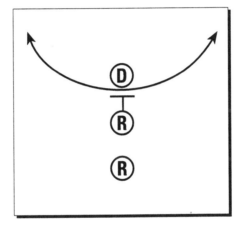

Drill #16: Swat and Swim Drill

Objective: To develop an effective release against tight man or tight rolled coverage.

Description: This drill involves two lines of players facing each other. One of the lines simulates defensive backs in close proximity to the offensive players. The players in the defensive line will assume defensive-ready positions, with their knees bent and their hands extended eight to 12 inches from the offensive players with whom they are paired. The offensive players in the opposing line will assume two-point positions. On verbal command ("Hut!") or the coach's whistle, the offensive player should slap away the rear hand of the defensive player and execute a swim release (arm over). The defensive player should try to extend his hands to the offensive player's chest. Receivers should execute three swim releases to the right and three to the left. When using a right stance and a left stance, both stances should be worked equally.

Coaching Points:

- Coaches should be able to see the hands of the receivers slap the hands of the defensive players.

- Receivers should get their arms over their palms and reach to the sky.

- The receivers should get their trail legs through on the release.

- All receivers should release in the same direction.

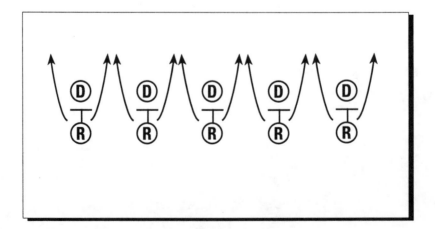

Drill #17: Swat and Rip Drill

Objective: To develop an inside release against tight man or rolled corner coverage.

Description: Two lines of players face each other. One line assumes defensive-ready positions while the opposing (offensive) line is in a two-point stance. Players in the defensive line will extend both hands in a position to jam the offensive players as they release from the line of scrimmage. From the two-point stance, the offensive player should execute a swat and rip move. The same move should be performed three times to the right and three times to the left.

Coaching Points:

- Coaches should see the hands of the receivers slap the hands of the defensive players.

- Receivers should execute a forceful rip-through.

- The receivers should get their trail hips and trail legs past the defenders.

- All receivers should release in the same direction.

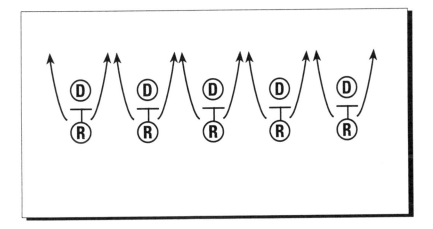

Drill #18: Swat Drill

Objective: To develop an effective release against tight man or tight rolled coverage.

Description: One line of players who are simulating defensive backs position themselves close to a line of receivers. Defensive players should be in ready positions, with their knees bent and their hands extended at chest level, about eight to 12 inches away from the offensive players. On verbal command the offensive players execute swat releases to either the right or the left. A swat release is when a receiver uses both hands to slap away the hand or the hands of the defensive player. This move, used when the receiver is having difficulty with the strength of the defensive player, allows the receiver to keep the defensive player's hands off him. Receivers should execute three releases to the right and three releases to the left. The players will then change responsibilities.

Coaching Points:

- Coaches should see the hands of the receivers slap the hands of the defensive players.

- After the swat, the receivers should get their trail hips through on the release.

- Receivers should be strong with their hands.

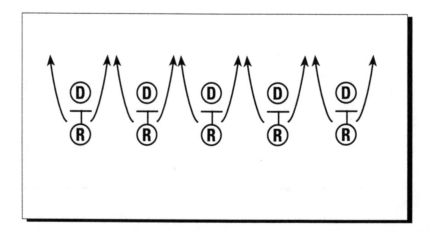

Drill #19: Burst Drill

Objective: To develop an effective release against soft zone or soft man coverage, along with teaching the receiver to close the cushion against the defensive coverage.

Description: Receivers should be aligned across a yard line in their two-point stances. On verbal command, each receiver, or the entire group, should accelerate for five yards by bursting off the line of scrimmage. The second phase of the drill has the receivers bursting off the line of scrimmage for 10 yards. The third and final phase has the receivers bursting off the line of scrimmage for 15 yards.

Coaching Points:

• Correct stance and explosion should be practiced.

• Receivers should use proper running mechanics.

• Receivers should use their top running speeds at five, 10 and 15 yards.

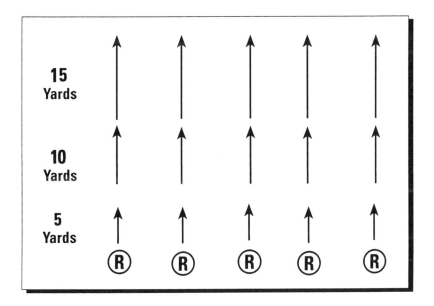

Drill #20: Inside Radical Release Drill

Objective: To develop an effective release against tight man or tight rolled coverage.

Description: This drill involves a release where the receiver attempts to avoid any contact with a defender playing the receiver tight to the line of scrimmage. The players pair up, one as a defender and one as a receiver. The defender aligns himself close to the receiver and assumes a defensive technique. The receiver aligns in a two-point stance. On verbal command, he will execute a very radical inside release away from the defender and try to avoid contact with that player. The receiver should perform three releases to the right and three to the left. The players should then change responsibilities.

Coaching Points:

- Receivers should execute a sharp inside release.

- Receivers should think about bursting off the line of scrimmage.

- The angle of the release is important.

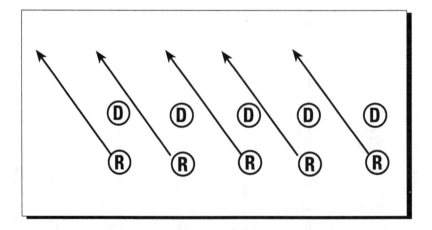

Drill #21: Outside Radical Release Drill

Objective: To develop an effective release against tight man or tight rolled coverage.

Description: This drill involves a release where the receiver attempts to avoid any contact with a defender playing the receiver tight to the line of scrimmage with inside leverage. Players pair up as defenders and receivers. The defender aligns close to the receiver and assumes a defensive technique. On verbal command, the receiver will execute an outside radical release from a two-point stance and avoid contact with the defender. The receiver should perform three releases to the right and three to the left. The players then change positions and responsibilities.

Coaching Points:

- Receivers should execute a sharp outside release.

- Receivers should think about bursting off the line of scrimmage.

- The angle of the release is important.

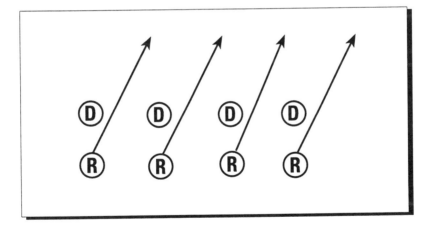

CHAPTER 3

ROUTE-RUNNING DRILLS

Drill #22: Snapping the Head Drill

Objective: To develop and teach the skills involved in running routes correctly.

Description: The receiver should snap his head and his eyes to the quarterback's hand as the receiver's foot is planted for an inside or outside break. This separation technique allows the quarterback to deliver the ball earlier. The receiver should first walk the route and snap left as his right foot is planted for a left break. He should first walk the route fast, then jog it, stride it, and finally run it.

Coaching Point:

- The snap of the ball and the planting of the receiver's foot should be simultaneous.

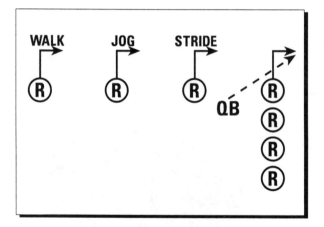

Drill #23: Out-and-Up Drill

Objective: To develop and teach the skills involved in running routes correctly.

Description: This drill involves a fake, and the key to the fake is the use of the head. On the out move by the receiver, the back of his helmet should be turned to the defender in the apparent act of looking for the ball. On the break upfield, his head should be turned to the ball only after running speed has been established. The receiver should move his helmet smoothly from the position of faking a look back at the passer to a position of looking for the pass. On the receiver's third step, after turning upfield, his eyes should be on the ball that is already in the air.

Coaching Points:

- This movement is similar to a weave at 80-degree angles.

- The out move can be performed with either three steps or five steps.

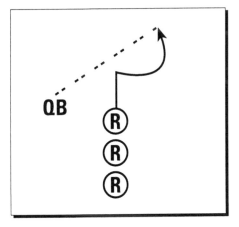

Drill #24: 90-Degree Cut Drill

Objective: To develop and teach the skills involved in running routes correctly.

Description: While running a route, the receiver should stop on the next-to-last step and use the last step to drive himself into a change of direction. The receiver should practice "fastening" his head on the quarterback by snapping his head around as his cleats are planted on the last step. The head should get around before the body. Receivers should make three 90-degree cuts in each direction.

Coaching Point:

- The receiver should try not to slow down until he puts his heel into the ground on the next-to-last step of the route.

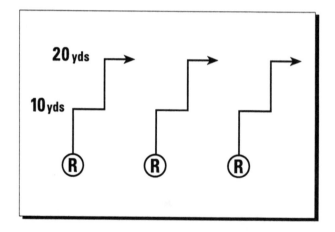

Drill #25: Change of Pace Drill

Objective: To develop and teach the skills involved in running routes correctly.

Description: Receivers will practice giving the appearance that they are running at full speed, when they really are not. This drill will test their ability to turn on their speed against defenders.

Coaching Point:

- This drill will teach receivers how to run at different speeds and further develop their faking techniques.

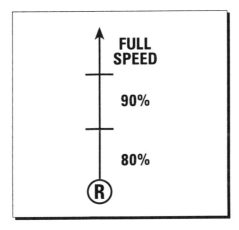

Drill #26: Stutter Fake Drill

Objective: To develop and teach the skills involved in running routes correctly.

Description: From a controlled run, the receiver should reduce his forward lean and rest on the toe of his back foot as if he is planning a pattern cut. This stand-up action and the foot stutter should occur at the same time, but it continues only for a moment. The action will initiate the defensive player's momentum toward the receiver, but as the defensive player reacts, the receiver should have already continued his deep pattern. Receivers should remember to stutter abruptly enough to force a reaction from the defensive player. The stutter occurs in the stick, after which the pattern can continue.

Coaching Points:

- The stutter fake is used to set up deep patterns and follows the same principle as the Change of Pace fake, where it draws in the defensive player.

- This fake is fast and works best when it comes after the receiver has just made a successful pattern cut.

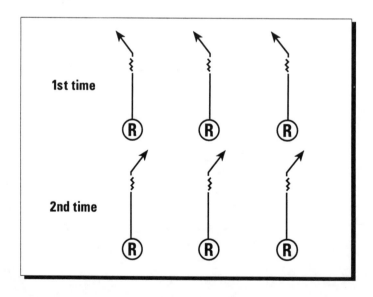

Drill #27: Direction Fake Drill

Objective: To develop and teach the skills involved in running routes correctly.

Description: The receiver should make a one-quarter turn and cut while he is running forward. The defensive player will have to make a half turn while he is running backwards, giving the advantage to the receiver.

Coaching Point:

- By accelerating his leg and arm action and angling just outside the defensive player, the receiver can cause the defensive player to get his feet crossed and turn in the opposite direction of the receiver's cut.

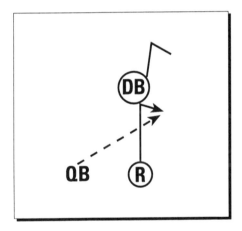

Drill #28: Approach Running Drill

Objective: To develop and teach the skills involved in running routes correctly.

Description: The coach will call out a pattern, and the receiver should run the route without catching a pass.

Coaching Point:

- This drill will teach receivers the proper running form required for faking.

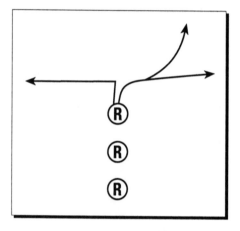

CHAPTER 4

BREAK-POINT DRILLS

Drill #29: Look Quick Drill

Objective: To teach a receiver to turn his head and shoulder first, before he turns the rest of his body and makes the final cut for the ball.

Description: The receiver should run an out pattern at five yards, and the quarterback should throw the ball as the receiver plants his leg for the break. This drill can also be used with a group of receivers standing stationary. On command from the coach, the ball should be thrown so that the receivers have to snap their heads and their shoulders around in order to see the ball and catch it.

Coaching Point:

- Coaches should stress the turning of the shoulder and the snapping back of the head.

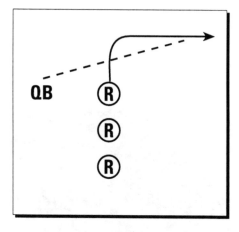

Drill #30: Breaking-Point Drill

Objective: To allow receivers to practice their various cuts.

Description: Receivers should practice a variety of cuts and concentrate on planting their feet and keeping their knees bent. The cuts should be made under complete control.

Coaching Point:

- Receivers should practice a wide variety of cuts (45 degrees right and left, 90 degrees right and left, etc.).

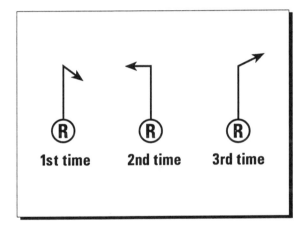

Drill #31: Kneel Pass Pattern Drill

Objective: To learn the pass patterns and how to run them correctly.

Description: Receivers should align themselves by formation in lines. Quarterbacks should stand where the center would normally be. On the quarterback's count, receivers in each line should run pass patterns. On completion of the passes, they should kneel where the passes are caught. The next line of receivers should run the same patterns. On completion of the passes or completion of the patterns, they should be near the kneeling receivers, and they will kneel themselves. The already kneeling receivers will then get back in line.

Coaching Point:

- This drill should develop conformity in pass patterns and stress where each route should end up when it is run.

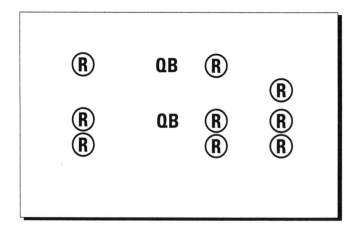

Drill #32: Break-Point Drill

Objective: To teach the receiver to use the proper cut at the break point.

Equipment Needed: One cone.

Description: Receivers will line up 10 yards from the cone. A receiver will then sprint toward the cone. At the cone pressure, he should perform a step and a stutter step and push off in another direction.

Coaching Point:

- The shoulders are the key. The receiver should put no arc or curve in his break, otherwise, the defensive player will be allowed to close the distance between himself and the receiver.

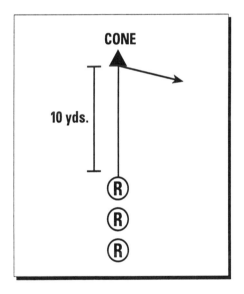

Drill #33: Five-Yard Square Drill

Objective: To teach the receiver to run at full speed while maintaining body control.

Description: Running at full speed, the receiver should "push" the defensive player with his head and eyes and then square back in to receive the pass.

Coaching Point:

- Coaches should start receivers from both sides of the field.

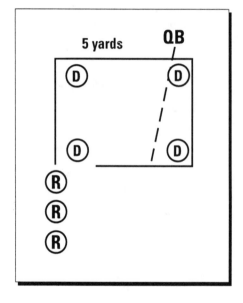

Drill #34: Find-the-Hole Drill

Objective: To teach breaking, body control, and catching.

Description: While running with a ball, a receiver should tuck the ball away and break in different directions.

Coaching Point:

- This drill also encourages a receiver to see how fast he can run while keeping his body under control.

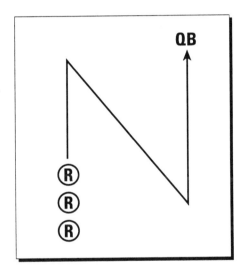

Drill #35: Curl Route Drill

Objective: To teach how to use the proper techniques at a route's break point.

Description: The receiver should plant his outside foot, whip his head and his shoulder around, and work inside and back toward the ball after it is thrown by the quarterback. Receivers should never remain stationary when the ball is in flight.

Coaching Points:

- Receivers should close to meet the ball.

- Receivers should try to fill the open passing lanes between themselves and the quarterback.

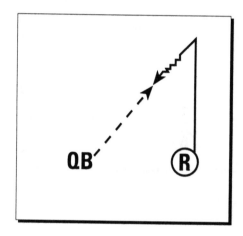

Drill #36: Post Route Drill

Objective: To teach how to use the proper techniques at the route's break point.

Description: The receiver should take a short step with his outside foot. The plant foot should be in line with the chin so as to achieve proper balance and maximum acceleration. The receiver should not round off the corner of the inside foot. The post angle should be kept thin, and the receiver should stay away from the inside safety.

Coaching Point:

* Against safety rotation over the top of the break, the angle should be changed to an "in" route.

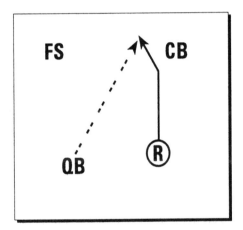

Drill #37: Streak Drill

Objective: To teach how to use the proper techniques at the route's break point.

Description: The receiver should find out early if he has greater speed than the defensive back. The receiver will run his route under the pressure of a defender. He can use a change of speed or he can "gather steps" to lull the defender and then break deep on him. The receiver should run a tangent line and make the catch after the quarterback throws the ball.

Coaching Point:

• Receivers should always release to the outside.

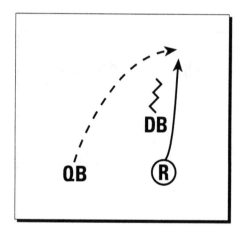

Drill #38: Three-Step Drill

Objective: To teach the most useful of all separation techniques.

Description: The first step is a skidding of the cleats or a 45-degree step to slow the movement of the receiver's body. The second step is a leverage step made with the foot well outside the body weight. The third step is an acceleration step in the desired direction, and it includes the snapping of the head and the eyes. A 90-degree turn in marching is also a three-step move, and so is the classic double fake, where the receiver fakes movement toward the direction he is breaking before he fakes and looks away from that direction. To let the leverage step get the foot well outside the body weight, the second fake of the classic double fake is made without a shift of weight.

During this drill the receiver should walk down a line, step 30 inches to the left at a 45-degree angle, and put his body weight over a point that is about 15 inches from the line. To put the foot in a leverage position, he should then step back on the primary line without shifting his weight. The receiver then steps 90 degrees to the left as he snaps his eyes around 225 degrees from their original direction.

Coaching Point:

- The receiver should be taught to control his balance point.

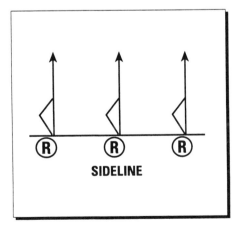

Drill #39: Route Drill

Objective: To teach receivers how to use the passing tree.

Equipment Needed: Four fake whitewall tires.

Description: The whitewall tires can be used as markers in a useful manner for the receivers. Marker 1 emphasizes a proper split. Marker 2 teaches proper release and emphasizes getting a head-up position on the defensive player. Marker 3 encourages the receiver to drive the defensive player to a depth of 12 yards. The receiver should make the defender turn and run. Marker 4 indicates that the ball should be caught at a depth of 10 yards as the receiver comes back to the ball.

Coaching Points:

- The receivers should run the patterns at full speed.

- All aspects of route running and catching should be emphasized.

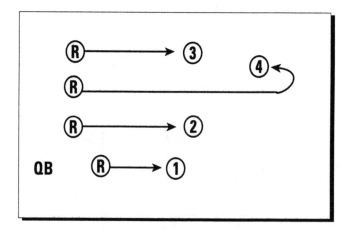

CHAPTER 5

STATIONARY CATCHING DRILLS

Drill #40: Catch-and-Tuck Drill

Objective: To develop eye concentration and the habit of putting the ball away each time it is caught.

Description: Receivers should play catch with each other and work on putting the ball away when they catch it.

Coaching Point:

• Receivers should catch, cap, and lock.

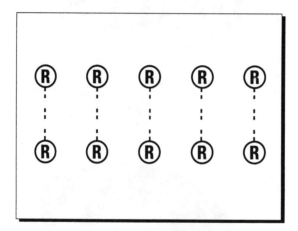

Drill #41: Scan the Sky Drill

Objective: To teach the receiver to locate the ball quickly and make the proper catch.

Description: The receiver should run in place with his back to the passer. As the ball is released, the passer should yell, "Ball!" and the receiver should find the ball and catch it in his fingertips. If the ball is above waist level, it should be caught with the thumbs together. If the ball is below the waist, it should be caught with the little fingers together.

Coaching Points:

- A quick head turn should be emphasized, along with proper placement of the hands.

- Receivers should catch, cap, and lock.

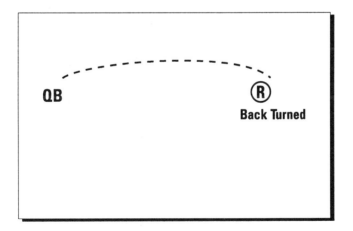

Drill #42: Pass Gauntlet Drill

Objective: To teach the receiver to locate the ball quickly and make the proper catch when he is being distracted by defensive players.

Description: Receivers form two lines for the quarterback to throw the ball through to the main receiver. They can do whatever they want to distract the receiver except touch the ball or the receiver himself.

Coaching Point:

- This drill is most effective when the ball suddenly appears "out of nowhere" a few feet in front of the receiver.

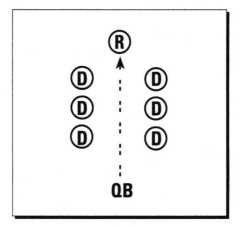

Drill #43: Scoop Drill

Objective: To help receivers learn how to catch balls that reach them just inches off the ground.

Description: The quarterback will throw several low balls to the receiver. The receiver should get low in front of the ball and present his hands and arms (with his elbows as close as possible) to the ball. When the ball strikes the hands, the receiver should elevate the ball and hug it to his body.

Coaching Point:

- The receiver can go through break-out, in, and hook motions; or he can just stand and face the passer.

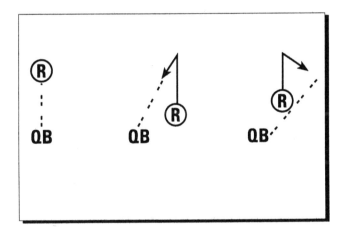

Drill #44: Split Vision Drill

Objective: To sharpen receivers' reactions and prevent them from making an unexpected jump.

Description: Instead of looking at the passer, the receiver should instead stand sideways and look off to the side. The receiver should be able to see the passer out of his peripheral vision. When the ball is almost to the receiver, the receiver should turn his head, locate the ball, catch it, and tuck it away.

Another version of this drill is called the Yell Drill. The receiver should line up in an out, bent-in, or back-to-the-passer position and look for the ball after hearing the passer yell. The passer should yell when he throws the ball. This drill will simulate a situation where the receiver breaks and turns after the ball has already been thrown.

Coaching Point:

* Snapping around the head should be emphasized, along with proper positioning of the hands.

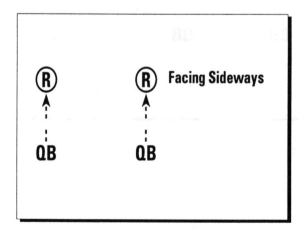

Drill #45: High Hook Drill

Objective: To teach the receiver to execute the hook and catch the ball on a high-thrown pass.

Equipment Needed: One net.

Description: With his back to the passer, the receiver should take one step, hook, assume the ready position, and react to a high ball. He should catch the ball, tuck it away, and pivot to the outside for a step or two.

Coaching Point:

• Receivers should time the jump and catch, cap, and lock.

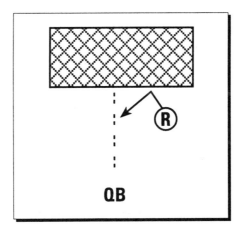

Drill #46: High Horseshoe Drill

Objective: To teach the receiver to make a reception by catching the ball over his shoulder.

Equipment Needed: One net.

Description: The receiver faces a net with his head looking over his shoulder. The passer should throw the ball high to that shoulder or over the receiver's head. The passer should then alternate and throw the ball to the other shoulder.

Coaching Point:

• The receiver can jog in place during this drill.

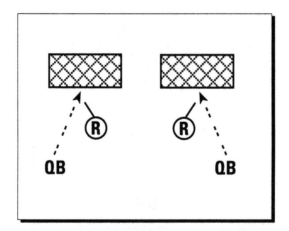

Drill #47: Quick Look Drill

Objective: To teach receivers to locate the ball quickly and make the catch.

Equipment Needed: One net.

Description: With their backs to the passer, receivers will, on command from the coach, turn to the right or the left with their heads only and make the reception over the shoulder.

Coaching Point:

• The receivers can only turn his head, and not his entire body.

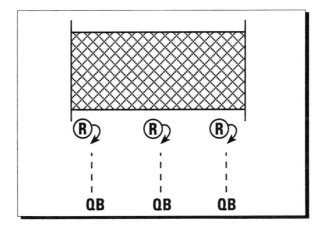

Drill #48: Clock Drill

Objective: To teach the receiver how to make receptions from different positions and with the ball thrown to different locations.

Equipment Needed: One net.

Description: The passer will throw the ball to the receiver at the 12 o'clock position and the six o'clock position.

Coaching Point:

• The receiver can take a stance facing the passer, with his back to the passer, or facing the passer sideways.

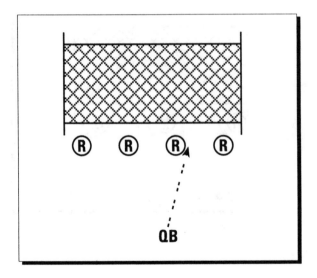

Drill #49: Quick Turn-Catch-Lock Drill

Objective: To develop the habits of snapping the head and the body around with great quickness, along with catching the ball with intense concentration and locking it away to prevent fumbles.

Description: The receivers will form a line and stand about arms' length apart with their backs to the passer. On the passer's command ("Left" or "Right"), the intended receiver will turn accordingly with great quickness, make the catch, and lock the football away. The passer may purposely throw the football before yelling the command for the receiver to turn. To increase the difficulty, the passer may also throw the ball high, low, or away to the side. The ball should be locked away with the web of the receiver's hand over the front point and back side of the football, and it should be securely tucked by the bicep muscle of the arm.

Coaching Points:

• To help with quickness, the receiver can whip back the elbow to the side when he is turning.

• The receiver should watch the football all the way into his hands and to the locked position.

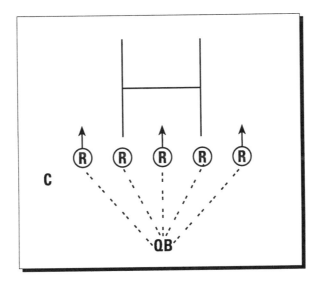

Drill #50: Soften the Ball Drill

Objective: To help the receiver use soft hands.

Description: When catching the ball, the receiver should begin to soften it on the first touch. He should then trace the path the ball would have taken had he not touched it. The final grasping part of the ball would be at the end of the ball's path.

Coaching Points:

- This drill should be performed with overemphasis and exaggeration.

- The receiver should follow every ball with his arms, hands, and eyes through the entire catch and path of the ball.

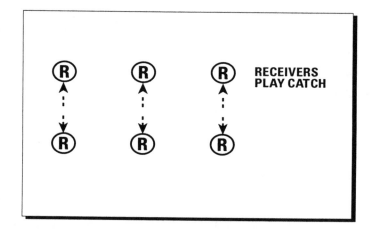

Drill #51: Harassment Drill

Objective: To teach the receiver to make the catch, even while he is being bumped and harassed by defensive players.

Description: The receiver catches soft 10-yard passes while he is being pushed from behind by a defensive player.

Coaching Point:

- This drill can be made even more difficult by placing another defensive player in front of the receiver and having that player hold his arms up in front of the receiver as the ball is passed. This defensive player should be five yards ahead of the receiver.

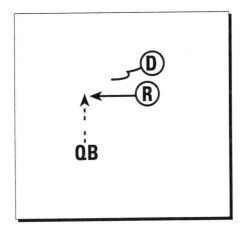

Drill #52: One-Hand Drill

Objective: To teach the receiver to make a reception even when he can use only one hand.

Description: The receiver should place himself sideways to the passer and jog in place to simulate running. As the ball is thrown to the hand on the side of the receiver's body, he should stop it by cupping his hand over the leading point of the ball. The receiver is not allowed to use both hands when catching the ball.

Coaching Point:

- The receiver can alternate hands by switching from side to side.

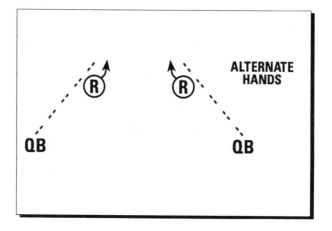

Drill #53: Tip Drill

Objective: To teach the receiver to make the proper adjustments and catch the ball when it is tipped by a defensive player.

Description: The receiver will position himself 20 yards from the passer and 10 yards behind a player acting as a linebacker. As the ball is thrown, the linebacker will slightly tip the ball, forcing the receiver to adjust to the deflected pass and get to the ball to make the catch.

Coaching Point:

- Receivers need to read the front tip of the ball in order to read the trajectory of the pass.

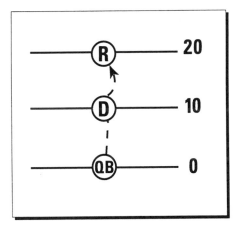

Drill #54: Knuckleball Drill

Objective: To teach the receiver how to catch poorly thrown passes.

Description: The receivers will play catch and try to catch five knuckleballs each. The way to throw a knuckleball with a football is to grab it by the end, with the hand turned opposite to the way it is turned when passing normally. The arm should be kept straight and delivered with a swinging sidearm motion.

Coaching Point:

- The receivers should be allowed to catch poorly thrown balls.

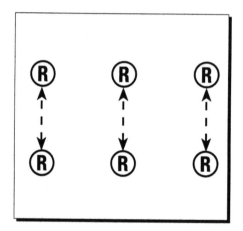

Drill #55: All Catch Drill

Objective: To work on the fundamentals of all five types of catches.

Description:

1. At a distance of 20 yards from the passer, the receiver should catch five passes with his thumbs pointing out.

2. Moving laterally at the same distance (20 yards), the receiver should catch five more passes, with his thumbs pointing in.

3. Facing the passer, the receiver should catch five passes in each pocket while imagining that a defensive player is behind him. He should move one or two steps toward the ball on each pass to separate himself from the imaginary defensive player.

4. The receiver should move in to a distance of 12 yards from the passer and scoop five passes that are thrown at his knees or lower.

5. Running at an angle away from the passer and keeping himself from getting too close to the ball, the receiver should experiment with handling overthrown passes with one hand.

Coaching Points:

• The receiver should secure the ball the instant it is caught on all but the one-handed catches.

• The receiver should use a low-shoulder position when he simulates running against defenders.

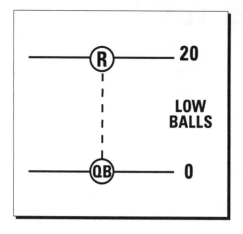

LOW
BALLS

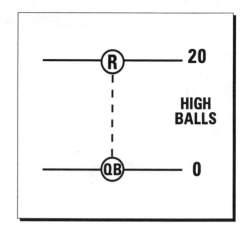

HIGH
BALLS

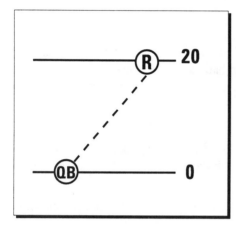

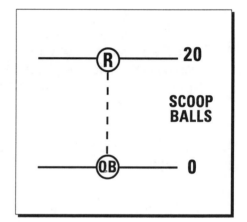

SCOOP
BALLS

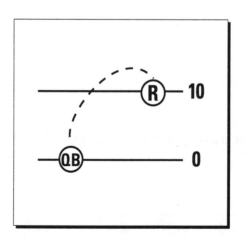

CHAPTER 6

MOVEMENT CATCHING DRILLS

Drill #56: In A Crowd Drill

Objective: To let the receiver use all the fundamentals of making the reception while he is being bothered and harassed by defensive players.

Description: Two or three defensive players should stand around the receiver and wave their hands in his vision, gently bump him, tip the passed balls, and generally bother him. The receiver should position himself about 15 yards from the passer.

Coaching Points:

- Complete concentration on the ball should be emphasized.

- The defenders should not be allowed to catch the ball.

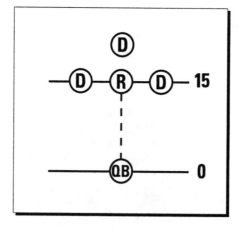

Drill #57: Pillow Drill

Objective: To emphasize catching the ball when a defensive player makes contact.

Equipment Needed: One air dummy.

Description: Three players participate in this drill—a passer, a harasser, and a receiver. The harasser should hit the receiver with an air dummy to stimulate contact. The receiver should concentrate on the ball and tuck it away when he catches it.

Coaching Point:

- This drill can increase the concentration needed for a receiver to catch the ball in a crowd.

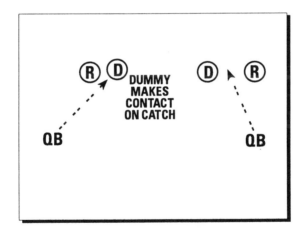

Drill #58: Leading Arch Pass Drill

Objective: To loosen up the legs and help in the development of eye concentration and speed control.

Description: The receiver should run 20 to 30 yards and catch the ball over his left shoulder. He will repeat the drill by catching the ball two-handed over his right shoulder. The goal for the receiver is to run his chest under the ball.

Coaching Point:

- The passer should emphasize arching the ball.

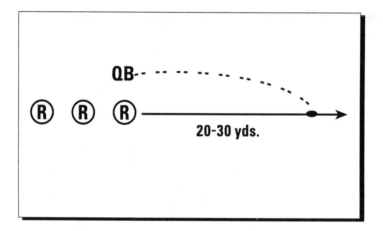

Drill #59: Wrong Shoulder Catch Drill

Objective: To teach the receiver to turn his head quickly and make the reception when the ball is thrown over the wrong shoulder.

Description: The receiver should run straight out from in front of the passer and look back over his left shoulder, trying to only turn his head. The passer should arc the ball over the receiver's opposite shoulder (the right shoulder). The receiver should turn his head quickly to pick up the flight of the ball and then sprint to make the catch. The drill should be repeated from the opposite side.

Coaching Points:

- The receiver should flip his hand when the ball drifts over the wrong shoulder.

- The receiver should not be allowed to backpedal around.

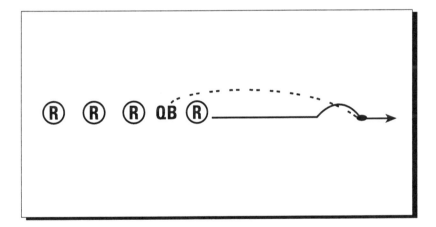

Drill #60: Hard and Behind Drill

Objective: To give the receiver practice on a type of pass, particularly the short pass, that frequently occurs in game conditions.

Description: The ball should be thrown hard and behind the receiver. The receiver should run and look at the passer over his shoulder. The ball should be thrown hard and to the opposite side (the opposite shoulder). Without taking his eyes off the football, the receiver should turn and pivot his body to make the catch. Proper footwork will be developed through repetition of this drill.

Coaching Point:

- Emphasis should be placed on quick reactions, flawless footwork, and good concentration.

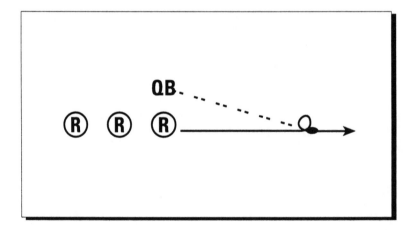

Drill #61: One-Hand Lead Catch Drill

Objective: To help the receiver develop the skills needed to make a one-handed catch over his shoulder.

Description: The receiver looks over his left shoulder and catches the ball with a right-hand lead. The receiver will be successful on this maneuver when he develops a "give" to cushion the ball. The drill should be performed from both sides.

Coaching Point:

• This drill serves as a particularly good way to help build up a weak hand.

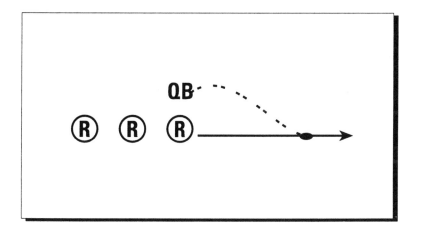

Drill #62: One-Hand Behind Drill

Objective: To help the receiver develop the skills needed to make a one-handed catch.

Description: With the passer aligned directly behind him, the receiver releases and looks over his left shoulder. As the ball is thrown (behind the receiver and above his hips), the receiver reaches back with his left hand and catches the ball with finger control, again practicing the "give" necessary to cushion the ball. The drill should be repeated from the other side.

Coaching Point:

- The receiver should gear down and open his hips and turn at the waist.

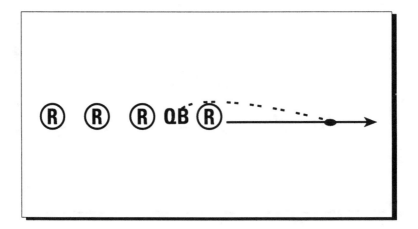

Drill #63: The Bomb Drill

Objective: To help the receiver practice the different ways of catching a long pass.

Description: The receiver will run deep routes and try to catch the ball three different ways.

1. One-Hand Lead Catch—Looking over his left shoulder, the receiver should catch the ball with only his right hand. The catch should be repeated on the other side using the left hand.

2. One Hand Behind—With the passer directly behind him, the receiver should release on the route and look over his left shoulder. As the ball is thrown behind him, and above his hips, the receiver should turn back with his left hand and catch the ball.

3. Over the Head—With the passer behind him, the receiver should catch the long pass by running under it. The passer should emphasize arching the ball to allow the receiver to run his chest under the ball.

Coaching Point:

*   All three long catches should be emphasized.

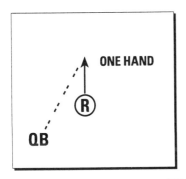

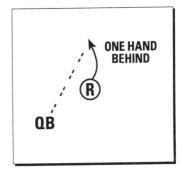

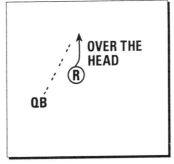

Drill #64: Zenith Drill

Objective: To develop the habit of catching the ball at its highest point.

Description: Often passes are thrown where the receiver has to catch it at its highest point for there to be a completion. That is the main reason to use this drill. Receivers line up at an angle to the goal post. One by one they should sprint to a point behind the goal post where they will catch the football at its highest point. The passer should throw the football high off the ground by throwing it over the crossbar of the goal post.

Coaching Point:

- Attacking the football in an aggressive manner and catching the ball at its zenith will most likely result in a completion, and even a touchdown, if the pass is in the end zone.

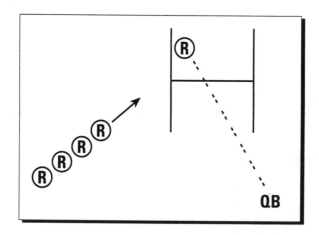

Drill #65: Square-Out Drill

Objective: To develop the technique of cutting at full speed and running a disciplined route.

Description: At a preferred distance the receivers should form a line perpendicular to the goal post. One by one they will run directly at the goal post and make a sharp square-out cut (not a roundhouse cut). The square out should be made by cutting a half yard before the goal post—at a spot marked by an object—and then bursting off the cut to catch the ball. The receivers should avoid contact with the goal post.

Coaching Point:

- When running the route, the receiver should place great emphasis on planting his inside foot, pushing off with the toes pointed slightly inward, and always flexing the knees on the full-speed cut.

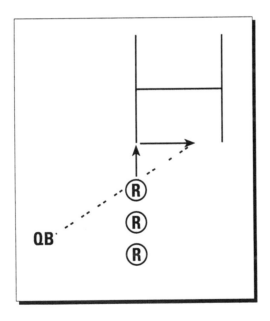

Drill #66: Sideline Drill

Objective: To develop an awareness of the sideline and concentrate on catching the football with at least one foot in bounds, or with the possibility of making a tight walk along the sideline for extra yardage.

Description: The receivers will line up facing the sideline about 10 yards away. The coach will start each receiver and throw the ball so that the receiver will have to make a legal sideline catch by dragging one foot in bounds. For the drill to be effective, the receivers should be sprinting and should know where the sideline is at all times and be able to keep one foot in bounds while catching the ball. A receiver should come down with the forward striding foot in bounds by dragging or pumping the foot to the ground as quickly as possible as he goes out of bounds. He should keep his eyes on the ball and catch it first, before worrying about the sideline.

Coaching Point:

• Receivers should learn to never look down, but instead "feel" where the sideline is through practice and repetition. Receivers do not want to get caught in the "Outer Limits."

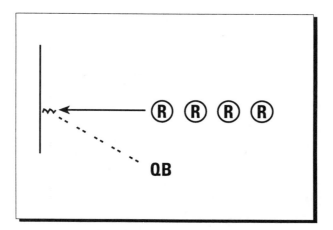

Drill #67: Comeback Drill

Objective: To develop the habit of quickly planting a foot and coming back toward the quarterback to catch the football, along with developing a quick cut and a burst upfield once the reception has been made.

Description: One by one the receivers should accelerate full speed off the line and make the appropriate cut to come back toward the passer to catch the football. Once the reception has been made and the ball has been tucked away, the receiver should plant and burst upfield to gain yardage.

Coaching Points:

- This aspect of receiving should constantly be practiced and emphasized. The receiver has to develop a habit of coming back toward the quarterback as the ball is thrown. The receiver should never just stand and wait for the ball to come to him.

- To gain an advantage over the defensive player and run a good route, the receiver has to maintain or increase the route by coming back for the ball. The receiver should not drift upfield, or the defensive player will recover and make up the ground he lost. Perfecting this maneuver will prevent many interceptions and broken-up passes.

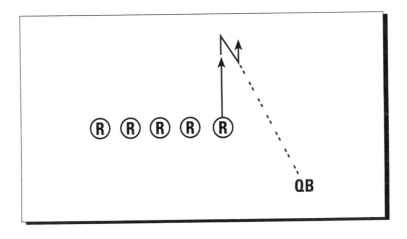

Drill #68: Tunnel Drill

Objective: To help the receiver's concentration when he is dealing with visual distractions.

Description: Two lines of receivers should face each other and stand between the passer and the receiver to whom the ball will be thrown. The lines of receivers will be waving their arms and the passer will throw the ball through this "tunnel." The receiver at the end of the tunnel will try to catch the ball despite the distractions.

Coaching Point:

•   The receiver should come back to meet the ball and have absolute concentration on the front tip of it.

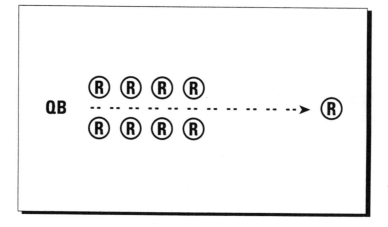

Drill #69: Bump Drill

Objective: To help the receiver's concentration when he is dealing with visual and physical distractions.

Description: One defensive player will stand in front of the receiver and wave his arms while a second defensive player will bump and grab the receiver from behind. The first defensive player may turn and bump the receiver instead of waving his arms. The receiver will feel that he is trying to catch the ball in a crowd and should stride between the two defensive players to make the reception.

Coaching Point:

- A third defensive player may be added to attempt stripping the ball from the receiver once the catch has been made.

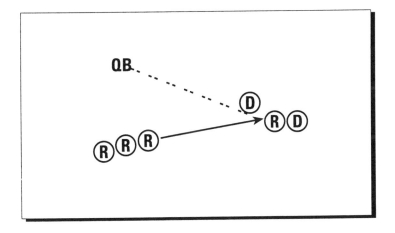

Drill #70: Bad-Ball Drill

Objective: To teach the receiver how to make receptions on poorly thrown passes.

Description: Receivers form two alternating lines. As a receiver strides out from his line, the passer will throw the ball in several different ways and the receiver will try to make the reception. He can throw the ball long, meaning the receiver has to run under it. He can throw a bullet pass. He can throw the ball immediately on the receiver's first or second step. He can throw the ball over the receiver's shoulder with a bullet pass or a high, soft lead. He can throw the ball short (in front hard or with a soft lead, and behind hard or with a soft lead). Finally, the passer can throw a banana ball, or throw it with a priceless wobble.

Coaching Point:

- These bad-ball drills can also be performed with the receivers running their routes.

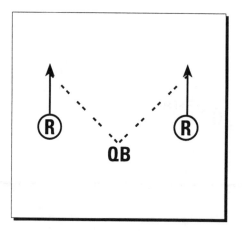

Drill #71: Concentration Drill

Objective: To help the receiver develop concentration and avoid the distractions he will face when he is trying to make a reception.

Description: Two lines of receivers work in opposite directions. The far line will be the receivers. Those in the near line will attempt to distract the receivers through their movement only. The passer stands 12 yards away from the receivers.

Coaching Point:

• The line providing the distraction should not change the flight of the ball.

• As receivers progress, this drill can be run at full speed.

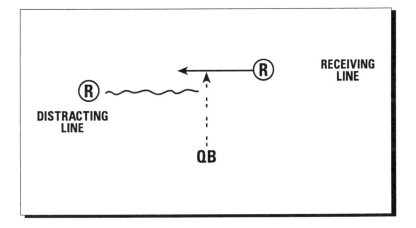

Drill #72: High Glance Drill

Objective: To teach the receiver how to catch a high ball.

Equipment Needed: One net.

Description: A receiver will run in place and be positioned four yards from the net. The passer will throw the balls high and in front of the receiver. Ten passes should be thrown to the left, and 10 should be thrown to the right. The receiver should catch the ball with his thumbs together and then catch, cap, and lock away the ball.

Coaching Point:

- The coach needs to emphasize that receivers should lock the ball away as quickly as possible.

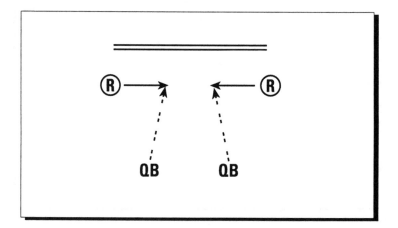

Drill #73: Low Crossing Drill

Objective: To develop the skill of running a crossing pattern and catching the ball when it is thrown low.

Description: The receiver should jog or run across the field. The passer throws the ball low and in front of the receiver. This catch is tough to make, and proper footwork is necessary for that to be accomplished.

Coaching Point:

- The receiver needs to bend at the knees and get his hands under the ball while preparing to use one hand as a stopper.

- This drill can involve the receiver actually diving for the ball.

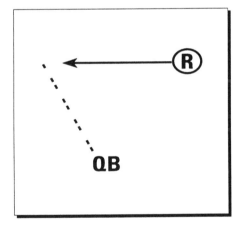

Drill #74: Stretch Drill

Objective: To develop the skill of stretching out to make the reception on an overthrown pass.

Description: The receiver will run flag, post, out and short patterns at full speed. The passer should overthrow the passes a little, and the receiver will attempt to catch the ball by stretching as far as possible. This drill can be started with the receiver jogging slowly in place as the passer repeats throwing the ball a little too far out of the receiver's reach.

Coaching Point:

• The receiver should be taught to accelerate to the ball while it is in the air.

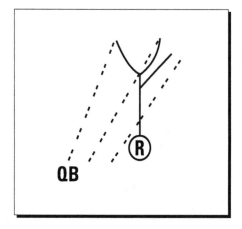

Drill #75: Endline Drill

Objective: To teach the receiver to use the proper footwork in order to keep his feet in bounds and score a touchdown.

Description: This drill is the same as the Sideline Drill, except the receivers are running toward the endline instead of the sideline. The passer is at midfield on the 20-yard line and the receivers are at a hash mark on the 15-yard line. A receiver will sprint toward the endline and look over his inside shoulder when the passer "pats" the ball. The ball is thrown so that it comes over the receiver's inside shoulder and reaches the receiver as he is leaving the end zone. The receiver has to catch the ball and work his feet to score the touchdown.

Coaching Points:

• The receiver should see the ball and feel the endline.

• The receiver should use shorter steps or a toe dance to keep his feet inbounds.

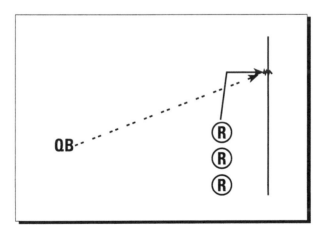

Drill #76: Corner Drill

Objective: To teach the receiver to work his feet and stay in bounds after catching the ball.

Description: The passer is at midfield at the 20-yard line and the receivers are at the 10-yard line on a hash mark. On the "pat" by the passer, a receiver will run a straight line for the deep corner of the end zone while looking over his outside shoulder. The ball is thrown so that it reaches the receiver as he is leaving the end zone, meaning he has to catch the ball and work his feet to score the touchdown.

Coaching Points:

- The receiver should see the ball and feel the endline.

- The receiver should use shorter steps or a toe dance to keep his feet inbounds.

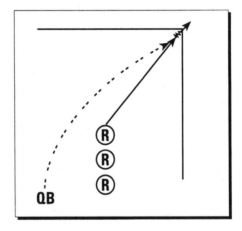

Drill #77: Crowd Drill

Objective: To practice catching the ball while going into a crowd.

Equipment Needed: Two air bags.

Description: The passer is at midfield and the receivers are favoring a sideline with their splits. Two defenders have air bags on their inside arms and are on a hash mark 15 yards down the field. The passer will throw the ball to the receiver as he reaches the defensive players. The receiver has to disregard his body and concentrate on the ball. It is a very tough catch to make.

Coaching Point:

- The receiver needs to have complete concentration on the ball and lower his shoulder after the catch to split the defenders.

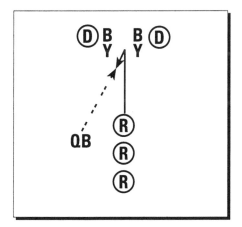

Drill #78: Lane Drill

Objective: To simulate situations where the ball may appear "out of nowhere" in an open lane on crossing patterns.

Description: The passer is on the hash mark and a group of four or five defensive players are stationed three yards apart on the sideline. The receivers are on one side and pass behind the defensive players. When the passer "pats" the ball, a receiver should sprint behind the defensive players and across the passer's face. The ball should be thrown between any of the defensive players. The defensive players wave at the ball, but avoid touching it.

Coaching Point:

The receiver should be able to catch the ball as it appears out of nowhere, and have anticipation on a crossing route.

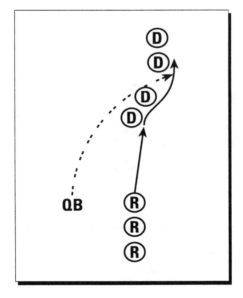

Drill #79: Roll-and-Catch Drill

Objective: To practice making the extra effort a receiver needs when he is knocked down and has to get off the ground and back into his route.

Description: The passer and the receiver stand five yards apart and face upfield. The receiver will sprint two to three steps from his stance, perform a forward roll, and come up running. The ball should be thrown on a short up route or a flag as the receiver is coming off the ground. The route is predetermined and the ball should come "out of nowhere" so that the receiver has to find it as he is coming off the ground.

Coaching Point: This drill will help the receiver learn how to get back up and into his pattern after being knocked down.

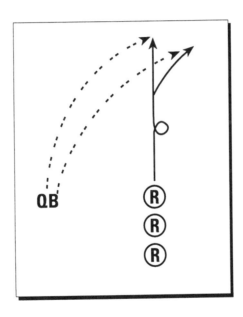

Drill #80: Maze Drill

Objective: To teach the receiver how to make the reception when he is being distracted by a defensive player.

Description: The passer stands at midfield, and a "maze man" stands eight to 10 yards down the field from him. The receiver will stand two to three yards behind the maze man. The passer will move up and down the line and throw the ball as the maze man moves his arms and occasionally tips the ball. The receiver has to concentrate on the ball and try to make the reception.

Coaching Point:

- The receiver should have complete concentration on the front tip of the ball.

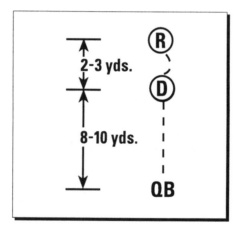

Drill #81: Hook Drill

Objective: To teach the receiver how to make the proper hook when he is being covered by a linebacker.

Description: A linebacker will cover the receiver, and the receiver has to curl wide or shallow, depending on the position of the linebacker. The receiver should fake in and go out, or "hook" in order to reach the ball and make the catch.

Coaching Point:

- The receiver needs to find the open passing lane between himself and the quarterback and come back to meet the ball once it is thrown.

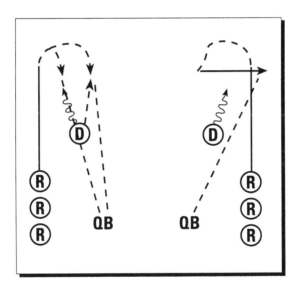

Drill #82: Challenge Drill

Objective: To teach the receiver to avoid the distraction of a defensive player and to stay on his pass route.

Description: A defensive player will harass the receiver down the line for about eight to 12 yards. The receiver tries to stay on his path and become acclimated to the defensive player so that he can make the catch.

Coaching Point:

- The receiver needs to learn how to be physical and stay on his route against bump coverage. He also needs to fight for the ball when it is in the air.

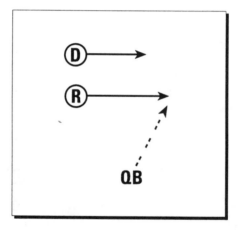

Drill #83: Alley Oop Drill

Objective: To help receivers develop the skills needed to make a catch on a high pass thrown into a crowd of players.

Description: Three receivers will position themselves down the field from the passer. The passer will throw the ball high in the midst of the three receivers, who will all try to catch it.

Coaching Point:

- The coach should be looking for athletic ability and the ability of the receivers to go get the ball.

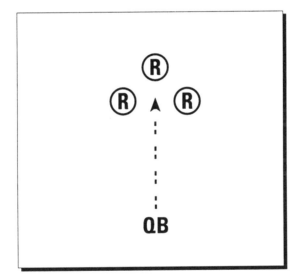

CHAPTER 7

RUNNING AFTER THE CATCH DRILLS

Drill #84: Ball Security Drill

Objective: To teach the receiver to put the ball away immediately after making the reception and before he starts running for yardage.

Description: After making a reception, the receiver should pick up and handle the ball with no air between his body and the ball. The idea is to cover the ball as fast as possible and get it into the carrying position. A defensive player can poke at the ball after the reception has been made and try to jar it loose.

Coaching Points:

- Proper technique in securing the ball should be emphasized.

- As receivers progress, defenders can be more aggressive in attempting to dislodge the ball.

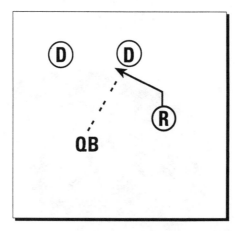

Drill #85: Out-and-Up Drill

Objective: To develop the receivers so that they will become aggressive and gain as much yardage as possible.

Equipment Needed: Several blocking dummies.

Description: The receivers should run a five-yard out pattern and be hit with a pass after their cuts. The receivers should then turn upfield along the sidelines. Defenders with dummies will try to knock the receivers out of bounds. Each receiver should dip his shoulder into the dummies and move straight upfield.

Coaching Points:

- The receiver should lower his upfield shoulder and attack the defender.

- The receiver can also be taught to use his inside arm on a rip move on contact.

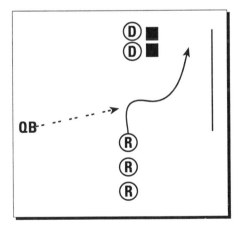

Drill #86: Shuffle-and-Go Drill

Objective: To develop a change-of-pace running technique.

Equipment Needed: Several blocking dummies.

Description: A quick hitch pass will be thrown to the receiver, who will catch the ball and then proceed upfield at full speed. As he reaches the first dummy, he should slow down or perform shuffle steps and then quickly return to full speed. The technique should be repeated at every dummy.

Coaching Points:

- The receiver should use one move and then go. Different moves should be developed, like the crossover step or the side step.

- The receiver should accelerate after the move.

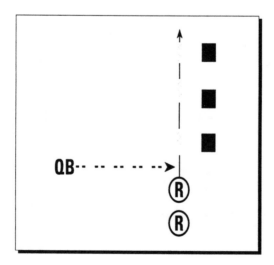

Drill #87: Gauntlet Drill

Objective: To help the receiver make a catch and keep his concentration while running through a group of defensive players.

Description: Two lines of players will line up facing each other and form a "gauntlet." The passer will fire the ball to the receiver, who will catch the ball and run through the gauntlet. This drill should be performed from both sides.

Coaching Points:

- The ball should be properly secured after the catch. The receiver needs to catch, cap, and lock.

- Defenders can become more aggressive as this drill progresses.

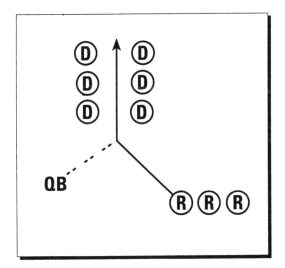

Drill #88: Open-Field Move Drill

Objective: To use the athletic ability of the receiver to avoid being tackled in the open field, and to develop the habit of turning upfield immediately in order to gain yardage after the football has been caught and tucked away.

Equipment Needed: Two blocking dummies.

Description: A defensive player will stand 15 yards downfield to attempt tagging the receiver with two hands once the reception is made. One by one receivers will accelerate downfield off the line to the appropriate depth and cut to catch the football. Once the reception is made, the receiver will attempt to avoid the defensive player by employing his open-field moves to advance the football. After the ball is caught, it should be immediately put away to avoid a fumble. The receiver then becomes a ball carrier and should try to gain every possible yard. Two dummies should be placed 10 yards apart to serve as boundaries.

Coaching Points:

- The down and distance to be gained for a first down are very important when the receiver is running. He should never give ground or give up a first down while he is taking a chance on gaining more yardage. The score and the game situation could make an exception to this principle, however. Possession and ball control should usually be the rule. Receivers should always be aware of the situation.

- The receiver should use the maximum of his athletic ability, along with head fakes, shoulder fakes, jab steps in the opposite of the intended direction, crossover steps, and other moves to gain that extra yard and possibly a touchdown.

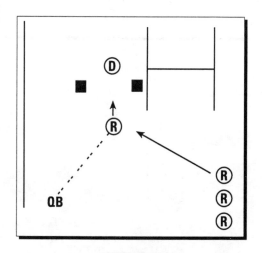

CHAPTER 8

BLOCKING DRILLS

Drill #89: Crackback Drill

Objective: To execute a crackback block on a defensive player in any of the three defensive areas.

Description: The receiver's shoulders should be parallel to the line of scrimmage and adjust to the defensive player's path or to the next defensive area. The defensive player applies the force. The blocking receiver should always stay under control. When he is in doubt about defensive penetration, the blocking receiver should react from the inside out. The block should be executed from above the waist for it to be legal. A pillow man can be set up in one of the three defensive areas to react to a sweep or an option play.

Coaching Points:

- The block has to be above the waist, and the head has to be in front of the defender.

- The receiver should adjust his angle of release in relation to the position of the defender.

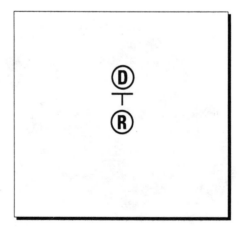

Drill #90: Blocking Mirror Drill

Objective: To learn how to block a defensive player by imitating that player's moves.

Description: The receiver gets face up on the defensive back and mirrors that player's every move. The receiver should be careful not to be overanxious and get through too early.

Coaching Point:

- The receiver needs to maintain patience on the block. He should keep his hips low and knees bent, and never overextend.

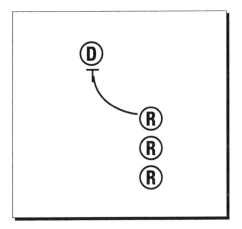

Drill #91: Shoulder-Roll Block Drill

Objective: To teach receivers a downfield block that they will use against the defensive secondary.

Description: On the snap of the ball, the blocking receiver springs for a point in the path of the defensive player who is going for the ball carrier. (Since the blocker knows where the play is designed to go, he can judge where the defender should be by the time that player gets downfield.) The receiver should take the flattest route possible so that he can get between the defensive player and the ball. He should never look back to find the ball carrier, but instead keep his eyes glued on the target. When approaching the defensive player, he should run hard but under control to counter any fakes. The receiver should get as close as possible to the defensive player, then throw a high block into that player and get his head and shoulders to the side of the ball. If the ball carrier is directly behind the blocker (receiver), then the blocker continues running until the defensive player commits. The defensive player should then be taken in the direction that the block is thrown. The block itself is a hard-driving body block. As the blocker nears the defensive player, he should throw himself at the defensive player, leading across with the arm opposite the support leg. The momentum of this thrust carries the other leg and the body upward into the defensive player. As the arm goes through, it rolls the shoulder forward, and contact is made with the near hip.

Coaching Points:

- The receiver should pivot, locate his target, keep his eyes open, and stay under control.

- When performing the block, the receiver should viciously drive through the middle of the defender. He should keep his head up, his hands into his body, and avoid lunging.

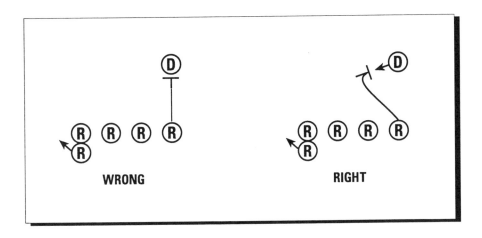

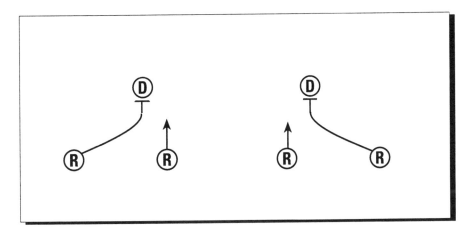

The receiver should keep running until the defensive player commits himself.

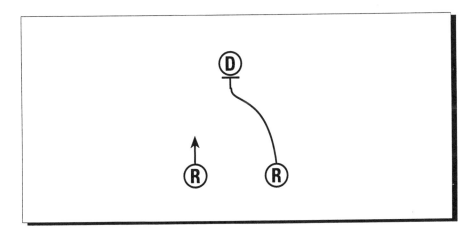

The block should be a hard-driving body block.

Drill #92: Block Defensive Back Drill

Objective: To learn the technique of blocking a defensive back. This drill is the accumulation of all the other individual blocking skills.

Equipment Needed: One blocking dummy.

Description: The receivers line up five yards in front of a player holding a blocking dummy. On command, a receiver will run at the player holding the dummy. The receiver will block and separate from him (bounce back) and then let that player start in one direction and block him again. The receiver should not attack him, but instead wait for that player to come to him. If the receiver feels he is losing the player holding the dummy, he should try to body block and roll. There are many ways that the player holding the dummy can try to run after initial contact is made. He can run upfield to the right or to the left. He can drift back right or left. He can even back up before initial contact is made and go right or left upfield at the receiver.

Coaching Points:

- The receiver should not lunge at the dummy.

- The receiver should settle before making contact, and at the time of contact he should keep his feet spread for a wide base and his hands close to his body.

- The receiver should be ready to block the man with the dummy any way that he moves, and block him as many times as possible.

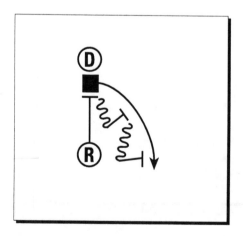 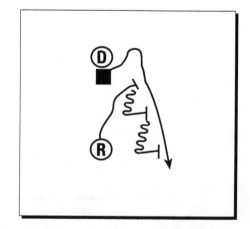

Drill #93: Hit-and-Recoil Bull Sled Drill

Objective: To learn the basic technique of blocking a defensive back. The initial contact or the first blow is stressed.

Equipment Needed: One bull sled.

Description: Receivers align themselves in two lines in front of the bull sled. From a football stance about one yard off the sled, a receiver will, on command, deliver a crisp blow to the bull sled and then recoil backward. After recoiling, the receiver will get back off the sled and settle in good football position. Variations include trying to repeat the procedure two times faster or running at the sled from about four yards out, settling quickly, and hitting, recoiling, and hitting and recoiling again. When running from four yards out, the receiver should not run right through the bull sled, but instead settle before first contact.

Coaching Points:

- The receiver should deliver the blow with his upper body, instead of striking with the legs.

- The receiver should keep his feet under him and his hands and arms close to the body. He should spread his feet and keep a good wide base.

- The receiver should not head butt the sled.

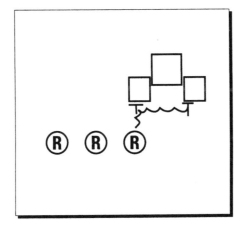

Drill #94: Hit-and-Recoil Shield Drill

Objective: To learn the basic technique of blocking a defensive back and to stress getting two hits on the defensive player.

Equipment Needed: One or two hand dummies.

Description: Two lines of receivers face each other about five yards apart. Two players in front of each line will be holding the hand dummies. On verbal command, the receivers approach the dummy holders and prepare to execute a stalk block. On whistle command, the dummy holders advance forward and the receiver has to execute the proper block. The dummy holder should continue to try to advance past the receiver, who will keep blocking until another whistle concludes the drill.

Coaching Point:

- Effort should be emphasized, and the receivers should be kept square to their respective dummies at all times.

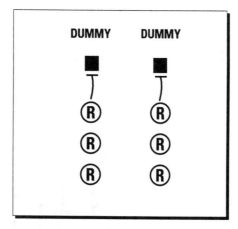

CHAPTER 9

SPEED IMPROVEMENT DRILLS

Drill #95: High Knees

Objective: To develop the muscles needed for a fast, long stride and to develop flexibility in the hamstrings.

Description: The receiver should drive his knees high and forcefully. When one leg is lifted, the other leg should be fully extended while bending forward slightly at the waist and keeping the back straight. The drill can be performed with or without the arms. When the arms are used, the elbows should be driven vigorously. The receiver should relax his face and arms and take quick one-foot steps.

Coaching Points:

*   The receiver should avoid lifting his thighs below a level that is parallel with the ground.

*   He should also avoid the following: Incomplete extension of the legs fully at the ankle, knee, and hip joints; leaning back; taking steps longer than one foot; and tensing the face and arms.

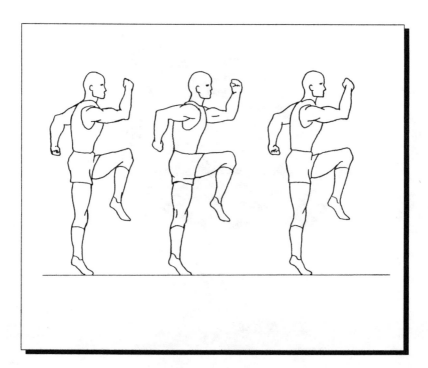

Drill #96: Footfire

Objective: To develop stride frequency and quickness.

Description: The receiver will move his feet as quickly as possible and bring the feet only an inch or two off the ground on each step. The toes should be pointed directly ahead with the weight kept on the balls of the feet. The receiver should think of only picking up his feet.

Coaching Points:

- The feet should not be lifted too high, and they should not be shuffled or have the toes angling out.

- The receiver should also avoid using arm action and tensing his face and hands.

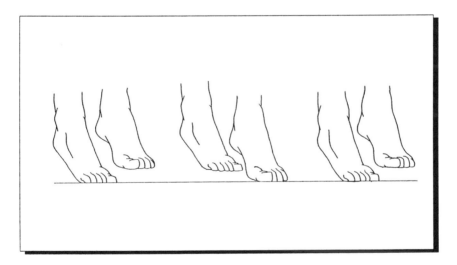

Drill #97: Ankle Flips

Objective: To develop explosive strength in the calf muscles.

Description: The receiver will alternately explode from foot to foot as high as possible by using only ankle action. He should land high on the toes and settle down to the heel, keeping the knees and hips rigid and the arms relaxed at the sides.

Coaching Point:

- The receiver should avoid the following: Achieving too much distance on each explosion, flexing the knees and hips, swinging the feet out to the side, and using his arms.

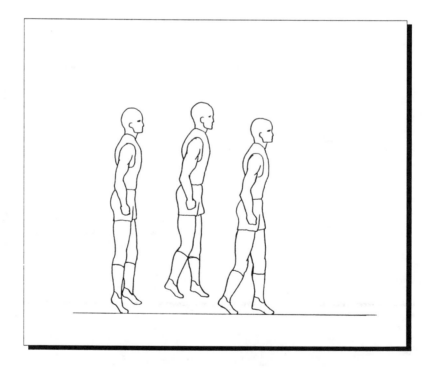

Drill #98: Heel Ups

Objective: To develop strength in the hamstrings and active flexibility in the quadriceps.

Description: The receiver alternately swings the heel of each foot to the buttocks. The action is a quick and smooth swinging motion produced largely at the knee joint.

Coaching Points:

- The receivers should be careful not to move forward too fast.

- Using the arms and lifting the knees by flexing at the hips should be avoided.

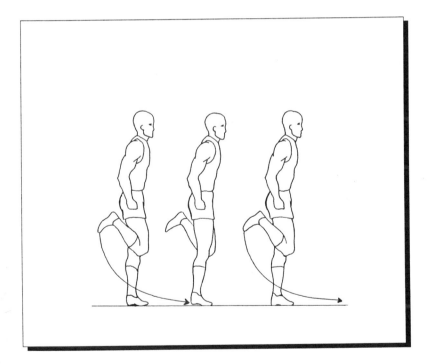

Drill #99: Harness Drill

Objective: To develop explosiveness and stride length.

Equipment Needed: One harness (A simple harness can be made with a lifting belt or even by tying a rope to each end of a towel).

Description: A receiver will be in the harness and a teammate will hold the harness from behind and provide resistance. The receiver will drive off the hind leg, extending completely at the ankles, knees, and hips. The leg should carry to the high knee, and the arms should be held at a 90-degree angle. On the backswing the elbows will be driven back and up. On the forward swing the hands come to the level of the shoulders, and the receiver should have good forward lean. His eyes should be focused 20 to 30 yards to the front.

Coaching Points:

- The receiver should avoid the following: Incomplete extension of the hind leg, low knee action, not driving the elbows back, bringing the hands above the level of the shoulders, and running upright.

- The receiver's partner should provide ample resistance.

Drill #100: Bounding

Objective: To increase stride length.

Description: The receiver explodes forward from one leg to the other and tries to achieve maximum distance on each stride. He should drive off the balls of his feet with his thighs coming parallel with the ground. The arms should be pumped vigorously in coordination with leg movements. The movements will be exaggerated, explosive, and flowing harmonious actions performed at one-fourth to one-third normal running speed. The receiver should also be sure to relax.

Coaching Point:

- Achieving too much height, going too fast, and showing tension in the hands, neck, and face should be avoided.

Drill #101: Arm Swinging Drill

Objective: To develop proper arm action.

Description: Standing with the feet shoulder-width apart, the receiver will place one foot 18 inches in front of the other and flex the knees slightly. He will bend slightly forward at the waist and keep his back straight. The arms will swing forward and back and be independent of the shoulders. The elbows will be driven back and be raised above the shoulders. The hands will come forward to the level of the shoulders. The arm motion should cause a bouncing action in the legs, and the receiver should be sure to relax.

Coaching Points:

- The receiver should not swing his arms across the body or keep the elbows at an angle greater than 90 degrees on the backswing.

- The receiver should be sure to drive the elbows back forcibly and prevent the hands from coming above the shoulders on the forward movement.

- The receiver should avoid tension in the arms and shoulders, and he should also avoid keeping his legs rigid.

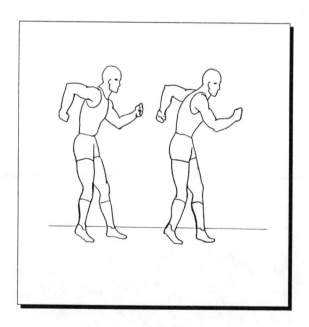

Stan Zweifel is the offensive coordinator at the University of Wisconsin-Whitewater. He has been a football coach for 24 years—the last seven at UW-Whitewater. During his tenure on the Warhawks staff, the team has achieved a 52-18 record. In the last four seasons, his offense has been nationally ranked in total offense, scoring offense, and rushing offense.

Prior to joining the coaching staff at the University of Wisconsin-Whitewater in 1992, Zweifel was the head football coach at the University of Minnesota-Morris, where his team won the 1987 NIC Championship and compiled a 22-18 record during his four-year tenure. He has also served as the offensive coordinator at the University of Northern Colorado, as the offensive coordinator at Mankata State University in Minnesota, and as the head football coach at Yankton College. Zweifel began his coaching career as a high school head football coach in New Ulm, Minnesota, where he coached for four years.

During his coaching career, Zweifel has produced 12 All-American players, as well as numerous All-Region and All-Conference players. He has also sent seven individuals on to play professional football. This past year, he was named the Wisconsin College Assistant Coach of the Year by the Wisconsin Football Coaches Association.

Zweifel is an accomplished speaker who has spoken at numerous football clinics nationally. He is a co-author of the best-selling coaching book, *Coaching Football's Zone Offense*. He has also produced several well-received instructional videos, including three volumes on football's zone offense—"Inside Zone Running Schemes," "Outside Zone Stretch Schemes," and "Play Action Pass Schemes."

Currently, he resides in Whitewater, Wisconsin with Diane, his wife of 23 years, and his children—daughters Saree and Shannon and sons Michael and Mark. Presently, he is working on another coaching textbook.

ADDITIONAL FOOTBALL RESOURCES FROM

COACHES ≡ CHOICE

- ■ **THE DELAWARE WING-T: THE RUNNING GAME**
  by Harold R. "Tubby" Raymond and Ted Kempski
  1998 •Paper• 164 pp
  ISBN 1-57167-166-8 • $16.95

- ■ **THE DELAWARE WING-T: THE PASSING GAME**
  by Harold R. "Tubby" Raymond and Ted Kempski
  1998 •Paper• 152 pp
  ISBN 1-57167-165-x • $16.95

- ■ **THE DELAWARE WING-T: THE OPTION GAME**
  by Harold R. "Tubby" Raymond and Ted Kempski
  1998 •Paper• 156 pp
  ISBN 1-57167164-1 • $16.95

- ■ **101 DELAWARE WING-T PLAYS**
  by Harold R. "Tubby" Raymond and Ted Kempski
  1998 •Paper• 120 pp
  ISBN 1-57167163-3 • $16.95

- ■ **101 DELAWARE WING-T DRILLS**
  by Harold R. "Tubby" Raymond and Ted Kempski
  1998 •Paper• 116 pp
  ISBN 1-57167162-5 • $16.95

TO PLACE YOUR ORDER:
U.S. customers call
TOLL FREE (800)327-5557,
or write
**COACHES CHOICE Books, P.O. Box 647, Champaign, IL 61824-0647,
or FAX: (217) 359-5975**

ADDITIONAL FOOTBALL RESOURCES FROM

COACHES CHOICE

◼ *101 QUARTERBACK DRILLS*
by Steve Axman
1998 • Paper • 128 pp
ISBN 1-57167-195-1 • $16.95

◼ *COACHING QUARTERBACK PASSING MECHANICS*
by Steve Axman
1998 • Paper • 80 pp
ISBN 1-57167-194-3 • $16.95

◼ *COACHING OFFENSIVE BACKS (2nd Ed.)*
by Steve Axman
1998 • Paper • 216 pp
ISBN 1-57167-088-2• $19.95

◼ *DEVELOPING AN OFFENSIVE GAME PLAN*
by Brian Billick
1997 •Paper • 102 pp
ISBN 1-57167-046-7 • $16.95

◼ *101 DEFENSIVE BACK DRILLS*
by Ron Dickerson and James A. Peterson
1997 •Paper • 120 pp
ISBN 1-57167-089-0 • $16.95

TO PLACE YOUR ORDER:
U.S. customers call
TOLL FREE (800)327-5557,
or write
COACHES CHOICE Books, P.O. Box 647, Champaign, IL 61824-0647,
or FAX: (217) 359-5975

ADDITIONAL FOOTBALL
RESOURCES FROM

COACHES CHOICE

BOOK:
■ *COACHING FOOTBALL'S ZONE OFFENSE*
by Stan Zweifel, Brian Borland and Bob Berezowitz
1998 • Paper • 184 pp
ISBN 1-57167-160-9 • $17.95

VIDEOS:
■ *FOOTBALL'S ZONE OFFENSE:*
VOL 1—INSIDE ZONE RUNNING SHEMES
by Stan Zweifel
1998 • Running Time: Approx. 90 min.
ISBN 1-57167-213-3 • $40.00

■ *FOOTBALL'S ZONE OFFENSE:*
VOL 2—OUTSIDE ZONE STRETCH SCHEMES
by Stan Zweifel
1998 • Running Time: Approx. 70 min.
ISBN 1-57167-214-1 • $40.00

■ *FOOTBALL'S ZONE OFFENSE:*
VOL 3—PLAY ACTION PASS SCHEMES
by Stan Zweifel
1998 • Running Time: Approx. 38 min.
ISBN 1-57167-215-x • $40.00

TO PLACE YOUR ORDER:
U.S. customers call
TOLL FREE (800)327-5557,
or write
COACHES CHOICE Books, P.O. Box 647, Champaign, IL 61824-0647,
or FAX: (217) 359-5975